MW00878792

# REDEEMED

Carolyn Faye Wilkerson

*Carolyn Faye Wilkerson,*
*a Redeemed woman,*
*living a transformed, brand new life today.*
*She was born the third child of six siblings, two*
*brothers and three sisters, born in October 1952,*
*in the state of Alabama. She has lived through*
*the lost of her mother at an early age. She*
*overcomes many setbacks in her live. She gave*
*birth to her son and lost mother within the same*
*year. She journeyed through a life of drugs,*
*alcohol and many death experiences, but she*
*has overcome. She has become a very*
*productivity woman and wants to be advocate*
*for women who are yet struggling with life's*
*setbacks and drug addiction. Carolyn Faye*
*Wilkerson, attending regularly at New Morning*
*Star Baptist Church, under the shepherding of*
*Pastor C.M. Manley. She has been born again*
*and has Jesus as her Lord and Savior. She is*
*employed as the supervisor of housekeeping at*
*the local hospital. She has been active in*

*many mentoring programs in the Lima*
*city schools, Big Brothers and Big Sister*
*and volunteer at a sober living facility.*
*Through heartache and years of*
*addiction she chooses to give back in her*
*community by sharing testimony. This*

*true redeeming story is her first written novel of many setbacks and tragic events that took place in her life. This is a new beginning in helping others. Carolyn Faye Wilkerson has suffered many losses. It was in the Year of 2001, she lost her first family member to different health issues; then continue to lose two more family members due to health issues. Such pain and tragedy to endure, she felt it and endure it. She lives today to help others find a way of life without drugs and alcohol. Her Vision is to establish recovery homes for woman and children who have suffered lose and who are bound in a life of drugs and abuse. Carolyn Faye Wilkerson lives in the city of Lima and loved by so many. Her family today is so important to her and they have a bond that grows deeper day by day. Her goal is to become a drug and alcohol counselor and address the issue in her community and worldwide one day at a time.*

# THE

# SIMPLE

# LIFE

It was a simple life that started In the Deep South of Alabama. I shall never forget what was once a simple life became a devastating, unforgettable journey deep rooted in my soul. Today I can stand tall and look high, high on life for I am redeemed, Jesus truly saved my life and I no longer fall into the low life of drugs and Alcohol. I am a recovered beautiful woman and Jesus paid the price that I have such a new amazing life.

 As I can recall memories of my life, before I recovered from the use of drugs. I remember my mom and family.
 My Mother name was Maple Lee Butler; She was a beautiful woman very strong, loving and hardworking woman. She dressed with elegance and style. Her smile and the glow of her face light up the room. Her hair was soft and long, she wore her hair pinned up in curls. She spoke with a soft voice, which was always pleasant to hear. She was a very stunning and amazing woman.

She never wore any makeup on her face, yet she was had a glow upon her that was very beautiful. She was more than qualified as a housemaid and she was very well respected woman. She provided for us the best she could and we never complain, we knew our mother loved us dearly. I had two brothers and two sisters; my oldest brother William he was nicked named (Pig), my younger brother James Otis (Bubbles) was his nicknamed. I'm the oldest girl, My Name is Carolyn Faye, and then Patrician Ann and then my other sister, Diane, sometimes called (Dee Dee). Then my baby sister, Sharon she was born later on after my Mom remarried.

My Mother was very protective of us and kept things pretty simple in our lives. Her first marriage was to man we never meet but he was our father, yet we later found out that he was just a man whom mom married to give us the same last name to keep us together; cause she was always keeping us protected.

Our baby sister she carried her Father's name "Boult" she spent much time growing up with him. We loved our sister even though she was not with us. Mom taught us to stick together no matter what we went through as a family.

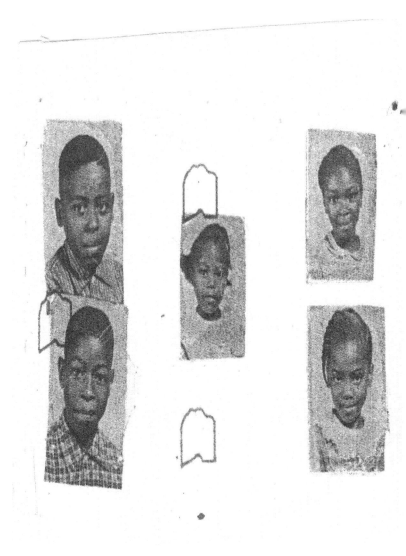

My Mother had six children I am the third child of sixth.  I have two brothers and three sisters, five of us were born in Florence Alabama, and one was born here in Lima, Ohio.  Before our life in Lima, My Mother was a single parent only two of us had the same father. My Mother did her best to provide for us she worked as a maid serving in home closer in the city.  She had to walk to work and sometimes maybe catch the bus.

My bothers had to watch us while my mom was at work:   Although we did not have much, things seem to work out and we didn't go without the basic things to survive on.  We had food shelter and clothes on our backs.  It had been hard for my Mother raising kids as a single parent, but with God's help and others family we survive.

I was born in October 1952, to me our life in Alabama was simple and this was where all people stuck together and helped one another. My brothers, I and my sisters we looked out for one another.  Our fathers were never in the household at all:  We had our mother and plenty of Love from her.  We were raised to respect and obey our mom and other adults in the neighborhood.  We lived in a two bedroom house, country yards with apple and pear trees. Sunday was family day, we had our favorite meal, fried chicken, fried potatoes with onions and green beans or pork beans with bacon. We watched TV. Or listen to mom's favorite music on the radio. We had a black and white T.V. but on day mom got us screen to show pictures with color and I remember we had an antenna with those rabbit ears to help tune in other channels, she would always try and make things better for us at home.

This was my favorite day with mom and the family; having Sunday dinner at home. On Sunday we also attend church with mom, she was a member of a community church in the city. Where we lived in our neighborhood it was made up of dirt roads, many of our neighbors had fields of farmland and gardens; they worked hard in the fields daily. It was all so simple living back then. Even though we didn't have much we were brought up to respect others and love one another. Life seemed to be good for us until things started changing within the family.

# MOVING

# AWAY

14

Mom had one brother, one sister and her father, who was my grandfather, his name was Milton Butler, this was all our immediate family, but before long we would be separated. Mom's sister had already moved and she was living in New York and then my mother brother, he moved to Lima from Alabama, now it was only my mom, her father and left in Alabama with us. It wasn't long after that my grandfather moved to Lima, now mom's siblings and father had all relocated to make life a better for themselves.

My Uncle got a job at general Motors, My aunt had married, she and her husband was now able to provide for her family in Buffalo, New York. My grandfather found a job and worked at the place called Ohio window cleaning. They had moved on and became very productive in their lives. Everything was still simple at home with my family but not for long.

As time went on my Mother and we continue our lives in Alabama. She still worked as a maid to put food on the Table; she provided the best she could. My uncle would visit from time to time with us, as we lived a simple life of poverty, this was a normal way of living for us, even though we need more we always knew our mother Loved us and she was doing the best she could.

Years had passed, it was 1960 and one day our mother told us we were moving now to Lima, Ohio. We were not happy to hear this, it was a shock, to hear this news, but we had no choice. Immediately the shock was over and we began to help our Mom pack within a few days my uncle was there to move us to Lima. We didn't bring any furniture we moved only with our clothes, I felt as we left everything behind, yet I wasn't old enough to understand why we had to relocated and move to somewhere else. I only knew my life was changing and the place I called home was home no more. The drive to Lima was 9 to 10 hours but to me it seemed forever. Finally we had arrived to Lima, we were not happy we left our home in Alabama.

Alabama had fruit trees in the yards; we didn't see these things here in Lima as we did in Alabama. When we arrived we had to stay with our grandfather in his apartment down the street from a bar. So many things were different from what we had been use too. As time went on e moved into our own place it was located in a different area of town. We began to adjust somewhat, our mother had got a job at the bar down the street from my grandfather.

# MOM'S
## PROTECTION

My mom was very protective of us and tried not to expose us to the lives to the different types of lifestyle that she serviced as a bartender. It was hard for her to keep us in the dark about things. Because we had lived a simple life and things were different in our surrounding and we saw that we were not shelter as we once was. There was a lot thing that had happened and our lives had changed in such a short period of time. We had now been enrolled in school and made friends in the neighborhood My Mom had met a man and our lives changed even more. This man was the father to my baby sister and later she married him. My baby sister was born in 1962 and everything seems okay for a little while. My mother was still very good to us; yet sometimes she had a few drinks. My stepfather was in the airforce, he also use alcohol, but he help provide for us and we became more adjusted to the changes in our life. We continue in school and things almost became normal for us. My mother and stepfather didn't always get along and we begin to deal with domestic violence in our home. I remember a time they would argue, real loud and I would hide my head with pillows so I couldn't hear them arguing. We had some good days and bad days we attended the community school. Our lives were a little bit better in Lima financially than when we lived in Alabama it was so simple.

Somehow the atmosphere had changed in our household but mom tried to keep us shelter and we could see that it was not the same. It was about to get worse and Mom would no longer be able to protect us.

It was one day after coming home from school. I'll never forget it because it was the day I found out, that the woman I knew as my mother had M.S. and was paralyzed from the waist down. It was in the year of 1963, one of the most traumatic events I'll ever remember changed my life.

We were still in school and my life had become very difficult. The woman I depended, I cherished and loved deeply in my heart was not the same. I was only 10 years old while trying to accept the change in my life.

Before we were ready to become young adults and teenagers, my bothers, my sister and I had no choice but to grew up and become responsible for one another. My oldest brother moved away, he went to live with his father.

Now my life became very hard while trying to accept my mother would not be the same. The woman that protected me and keeps me safe no longer was able to protect us. My mother was diagnosis with Multiple sclerosis which is an autoimmune disease that affects the brain and spinal cor. Mom was paralyzed at the age of thirty-six, her legs was drawn back to her hip; she no control over her movements. We had to learn to care for our mom; this disease had token control over mom's body. It was not much one could do during this time, medicine and treatments were very limited. During the time we spent with our mom she would always say, "If the Lord's will "as we made plans for each day. She would encourage us with her jokes when with bathe her and give her daily care. We feed her and we were taught how to turn her every two hours. We stayed in our home and attend school which was okay; we had Nurse Association care services visiting mom 3 to 4 days a week and they were very helpful. The nursing serve treated us good; bringing us food and preparing our meals, teaching us how to care for mom. We all had a part to do

and yes we went to school under all these
condition and we never had a problem caring
for our mom but this was traumatic changes in
our lives.   We loved our mother dearly; we
had to grow and become responsible quickly
during this time.

# *Wrong Choices*

Our lives weren't like other children in the neighborhood who went to play after school activities. We had to go straight home and care for mom and we did okay with this but some of the choices that were made changed our lives greatly.

Our stepfather stayed around but after while that was short lived. My mom was not the same women he married. He started spending time with some other lady from the neighborhood. He was having an affair with her. My sister and I found out who she was and where she lived. One day we caught him and her together. We were so hurt and we told our mom. She confronted him and after that he left and they were divorced. He married the woman he was having an affair with from our neighborhood.

Time goes on and mom's condition gets worse. My life is changing more and more. I am now in high school, I had a boyfriend or two. I recall some things that started to bring more changes in my life. It was the first time I smoke weed.  I was at school in the bathroom and at this time my mom didn't know what changes had started taking place in my life.   If my mom knew she would have been very disappointed in me.  I had become sexually active; I had grown up and became a young adult at life. Even though I spent most of my time at home caring for mom; I still became sexually active and even began smoking weed. I remember a couple of times I was allowed to go to the local playground; there I would meet my boyfriend. I spent time with him in school and afterschool coming me home.

As time went on my Mom was going in and out of the hospital.  I spent more time with my boyfriend, this continued on and during this time I became pregnant.  Another wrong choice without protection, I made in my life. I was only 16 years old in the 7$^{th}$ grade.  I didn't tell my mom; I didn't tell anyone.  As I got further along in the pregnancy, I couldn't hide it no longer.  My Physical ED. teacher, said "I notice you are not as active in the gym classes", then she asked "Are you Pregnant?  I said, "Yes" she told me to go and see the guidance counselor.   I then made an appointment to see the guidance counselor.  I told the counselor I was pregnant, she asked me had I told anyone about this and I said No.

She told me I couldn't continue in school being pregnant; I needed to tell my parents.
I went home to tell my mother why I was no longer in school.  It was the hardest thing I ever had to do because I knew she would not be happy.  When I told my Mom I was pregnant she didn't say nothing she just looked at me and begin to cry.  I could see the disappointment all over her face.  My Mom never yelled or made a sound, I wished she would have yelled or screamed at me but she didn't.  The look on her face was enough to tell me of her pain. It was one of the worst times in my life.

# Giving Life and taking Life away

It all was happening so fast, I could get back to simple life, I didn't want to grow this fast I had no idea how my life was about change and devastate me for the rest of my life.

I was getting closer to my time of delivery and my mom was getting worse. I wanted this all to be over, not knowing my life was about to change drastically again. I had so much confusing going on within me because of what I had to face and how would I get through?

It was June 25$^{th}$, 1969, my mom was in the hospital that day and I was going into labor. My sister ran out to tell the neighbor, I was having the baby and needed to go the hospital. She called my aunt and she came while I gave birth to a baby boy. My sister told my mom I had a boy and my mother told me to name the baby "Ricky", so that's what I named him.

My Mom went home from the hospital and I went home a week later.


At home with Mom and a new born baby, I had to learn how to be a mother and care for a new born baby and caring for my mom who was ill. I was not able to return to school at that time.

My mom had been sick for 6½ years and now on Feb. 14$^{th}$ my mom had passed away. I was only a teenage girl at 17$^{th}$ with a 6 month old baby boy.  My sisters were 14 and 13 years old without a mother. It was the next morning after the funeral and all the immediately had truly left us, except our grandfather.

I remember mom's sister taking things that belong to my mom, I didn't understand why. She took things such as, mom's jewelry, fur coats and clothes; mom was a well dress woman and had very elegant clothes and expensive jewelry.  I remember this special bracelet she wore, it opened up with her picture and special words were in graved inside. She even took my mom's wedding rings but later on they were given back. I know I didn't understand at that age what was going on and why auntie took mom's belongings from our home.

No one knew how frighten we were at this moment, I thank God for the neighbor who came to help and comfort us during this time. It was the darkest and hardest time of our lives, after burying our mom and everyone was gone. It even became the scariest moments of our lives.  We were all alone without mom. Our grandfather had to come live with us, my oldest brother was married with children living in Virginia; he had to returned home with his family.

Now it was only my two sisters, my one brother; me and my baby with our grandfather who was up in age living in the home. Then somehow children welfare found out about my grandfather being the only adult in the house with us. We were soon notified that grandfather no longer could keep us and we had to be taken out of the home.

God had a guarding angel in the Neighborhood. There was a mother in the neighborhood willing to take my two sisters, me and my baby. My baby sister went with her father; my brother got his own apartment. After while I apply for government assistance; I was accepted for welfare and got my own place. My sisters were okay and they finished school but I didn't return back to school at that time. Time had passed and finally my sisters were of age. They both got jobs and my baby sister was still with her father.

My brother also was working but as for me I was on welfare with my son. Eventually we all moved in with our brother, but it was all for a short time.

# WHO AM I

No long after living with my brother was engaged and became married. Our lives had changed again and I was drinking and using drugs more now than I was in High school. I had a job at the local bar in town; it was one of the ways I was able to pay for my drugs use. I was always well dressed at work; I wore nice pantsuits and dressy shirts with sandals. I keep quiet and served customers with a smile. It was always a good crowd and good music playing; my favorites were Teddy Pendergrass, "turn out the lights, Frankie Beverly "Maze", Spinners, O'Jays, and Ale Green and many more. I liked my drink. , tangerine Gin with ice it was always good nights. I had a relationship dating an older guy that I could get even more drugs of choice through him. Whatever I could get high on; I used pills, acid, cocaine and heroin. I was not just taking pills and other drugs, I was shooting them in my veins, I was out of control but just didn't have the courage to admit it.

I thank God that my sisters were there to take care of my son. I was in this place, in my life where nothing mattered to me. I just wanted to escape from all the pain and drugs was the way out for me.

When I became an addict I became very selfish and wanted to stay out of touch with everyone. I didn't have to deal with life at all. I remember the first time I wanted to try Heroin. I saw a friend when she was shooting herself up in the arm and she begins to nod out, it was as though she didn't have a care in the world. Immediately my thought was that is what I wanted. I wanted to be out of touch with reality. I thought I could get away from all the pain that I was in. Now look at me I am a person on a road of disaster and destruction. I remember a time, when I met this guy and he was selling weed. After some time has passed he asks me if I would be interested in selling some weed for him. Wow of course I said yes, but this was not a good Idea because I only smoked up his entire weed by myself. When the time came for me to give the guy his money for the weed I suppose to have sold, I didn't have his money nor did I have his weed. I tried to avoid him, he started questioning my sisters, and he came to their home where my son lives. My sister told me the guy came looking for me; he said he was going to kill me if I didn't give him that money. I then stayed away from home because I was so scared and very afraid.

It was one night I was partying at the club having a good time, I turned around there he was with a gun in my face. There was another man with him and the guy with the gun said to me come on "B" we're taking a ride. My whole life flashed before me and I knew in my heart that he was going to do something terrible to me. He proceeded to push and shove me out the door. It was a club full of people, but no one noticed what was happening to me. As we reached the door to exit the club, there stood my brother outside of the club. My brother got in between me and guy, the guy said let me go he had a matter to take care with me. The devil tried to kill me that night but God had another plan for life. I was not aware of God's plan for me at that time. God spared my Life and he has spared my life many other times. After this particular incident my life with drug use had escalated to using the harder drugs.

It was a big hole in my Heart; I missed my mom so much. There's no love like a mother's love. I had then moved to Tennessee with some friends. My drug addictions lead to a shameful life while in Tennessee. My drug use had gotten worse, I began to shoot up in my arm more. It was one time when I was getting high; I didn't know how strong the heroin was so I thought I was getting cheated on the amount given to me. Therefore I wanted to shoot more so I got more; as I was given more of this drug as felt myself getting weak. I started to buckle in the knees. I could hear but suddenly I thought i couldn't hear the voices around me. Then I heard my friend say take her outside and move her around so she doesn't pass out. I came around; I didn't pass out. I stayed in Tennessee and continued to use drugs and abuse myself.

A few years had passed; I was still in Tennessee, my sister were the caregivers to my son. They would send me money at times and show there love and concern for me. I thank God for my sister they took care of my son during the whole time of my addiction they were always there for him. I finally moved back home for good from Tennessee.
I moved back home with my sisters; my life was still consumed with alcohol and drugs, my life was not back on track. I was able to get my job back at the local bar around town. It seems like things would never change, I was in another death situation because I was out of control. God keep me from death again and I didn't understand at all.

# ROADS
# OF
# DARKNESS

I recall going to Mansfield with a friend of mine.  As we traveled the roads we were heading to the mall to do some boosting, which is stealing.  We stole clothes to sell for drugs. There were four of us, three guys and myself. We had to split up, so we wouldn't look suspicious.  We all were to meet back at a certain spot on the roadside, where we all had agreed to meet.

After about an hour and half, me and the person I was with; we return to the meeting area by within the mall.  There was no one there so we turned back and started looking for them throughout the mall, but we never found them.

As we continue to walk down the road we came to conclusion they were gone and nowhere to be found.  So we journeyed on. Before long some guy on the road pulled up on us and asked if we needed a ride.

We jumped into the car only to find out it was the wrong thing to do.  We found out this guy was a criminal and we no idea what he was capable of doing.  He took us with him to this house and told us to come in with him.  As we are getting out of the car I continued to watch him and our surrounding.  He stood up about 6ft. tall, very fair skinned with green eyes. His voice was soft-spoken and his words were well-mannered. He wore blues Jeans, white T-shirt and tennis shoes.

But all of sudden as he approached the truck of the car his whole demeanor had changed, he opened his trunk and pulled out a gun, everything then went wrong. I was now scared and concern about my life. He knew the guy in the house because he let us in, but the guide was blind; they made us sit down as they went upstairs. We later on found out, he was the caretaker of the guy and we were in his home and we had no idea what was going on. A little while later he came down stairs in a hurry and said lets go, I just robbed this guy; we had no choice but to go with him. We had no idea where we were at or where we were going. He pulled over on the side of the road; he had a shot gun beside him where we could see it. We were taken somewhere to an open field on the side of the road in the country. Then he told my friend to get out of the car, he had the gun now holding in his hand. My friend got out and he made him leave; he looked at me and began to cry as he walked away and then I saw him run.

We the gun still in his hand, I thought to myself here I go putting my life in death hands once again. My addictions continue to destroy my life as I travel this path. I was then told to get in the back sit. After getting in the back sit he begins to rape me, as he held me at gun point. My Life flashed before me once again. After raping me he made me get back in the front seat.

We pulled off, then I heard the sirens, I was now in a high speed chase and I could see the police coming behind us. We were going at a high speed and the police couldn't catch him. He had out run the police. I was raped and violated by this man but I was relieved I was still alive.

I realized my friend had made it to the police and told what happen, but at this point I was just thankful for my life.

Now that the chase was over and the police was no longer in sight, this guy said he would take me to the motel and he would be back in the morning. He let me out on the corner and then I went to the motel scared out of my mind. I stood to see if he was coming but he didn't, thank God. I then ask the hotel clerk if he would call the police for me and he said yes. I told the police officer over the phone what happen, he asked questions of where I was at, I told him where I was; he said you are next door to the police station so I walked next door.

I felt humiliated, scared and violated, but I was still alive. When I got to the station I told the officer from the beginning what happen, he said my friend had flagged them down and told them also what had happen.

They said were aware of this man that had been robbed; he was robbed by his caregiver, who was hired to work in his home. Little did I know that my friend had been arrested and now they were about to arrest me. I was told they could hold us for 72hrs or until they complete their investigation. I gave the police a description of what this guy looked like; they asked about the area were we where. I told the officer what I could remember and that we weren't from Mansfield. I told the officer I was from Lima. I asked to make a phone call. I called my brother, I told him part of what happen and I was in Jail.

My brother contacts a lawyer from Lima. I told him I had to spend the night in Jail; he said he would come and get me out of jail tomorrow. The next day I was released, the officer also informed the guy who had violated me and done that robbery had been caught. He also had robbed someone else and they identified him. My brother came to pay the bail, for me to get out and the officer released me; I was free to go.

It was a very quiet ride all the way home; my brother never said a word to me all the way home. I put my family through so much pain and heartache. Even though my life was spared, the rape and violation I experienced diminished my trust in me. Therefore I had built up a wall and I wasn't engaging in any meaningful relationships. Maybe if I would have gotten help or some counseling I could have responded different and made better decisions. I put my family through so and they still stood by my side and raising my son and being my safety net.

As I continued down this road of destruction my drug use became more and more a problem and I was so disappointed in myself. As my sisters continuously raise my son and caring for him, I would steady fall deeper into the drugs. I couldn't pull myself out; it was a new drug out called crack cocaine. It was like a new fashion designed and everybody wanted, so guess what; I did too. I tried it and I liked it very much. I had a new high with my old high and this was a recipe for complete disaster. This crack cocaine would make you feel like you could do anything while on your high. It would spread like wild fire, you be caught up in it and couldn't get out. You would be up for hours and days maybe weeks chasing the high like a fire gone wild. In my clouded mind I thought I was in control, but all the time I was out of control and didn't even know it. This drug crack cocaine seems to give me courage to chase this high by any means necessary. I realize I missed out on a good and normal relationship with my family. I missed the life that a normal person should live; functioning in a productive manner. I wanted to be normal and enjoy life but I couldn't overcome my addictions. I continue to be selfish walking into this darkness; going further and further into my addiction. I didn't consider anyone, not even the harm I was doing to myself.

Who is this person I had become? Where is the real me? I wanted to be me; I know you are in there somewhere please reveal yourself to me. I cried, LORD PLEASE HELP ME, as days, weeks, Years went passed. I was dying in this addiction and I needed help. I wonder sometimes what was going to happen what it would take. I wanted to be free what must I do? I missed out on all the important things of my life and I missed out on my son growing up

in his youthful years.   My heart was breaking
remembering all these things but this
addiction still had a hold on my life.  Again
what can I do to get free?
Is there any hope for me? I could only wonder
was any hope left for me. Time had passed and
my sister that was older than me had gotten
married; she said she had to let me go, it was
the hardest thing she had to do.  She couldn't
support me anymore.  She couldn't be the
safety net anymore after all these years.  Now I
could feel my safety net slipping away from
me.

I still had my other sister there for me we continue to live together, but it was only for a little while and she began to cut away from me; though we still lived together. I wasn't for long, she had gotten pregnant and had twins and then later she moved out and got married. Now it was just me and my son. I was mad at my sisters for leaving me, because my safety net was gone and was trying to find my way. I had to move out into another place. I moved into another place, I was on the program for met housing; my son attended high school. I began babysitting for my sister's twin boys; yes I was still getting high but not as much. I wouldn't get high while I was babysitting nor around my son. I would make sure my son was not at home or I would go over a friend house. I did all I could to keep him away from my addiction.

My son had friends in the neighborhood and sometimes he would stay overnight. Even though I did get high around him my son started drinking and I was not pleased. I let him know I didn't approve of his drinking. We both continued on with our negative habits, soon my son became a father, just as I became a mother at an early age. My son was the father of twins a boy and a girl. Sadly to say the boy only lived a few hours. Then after 18 months the girl twin had passed


My son life had become a pit of darkness, his pain and sorrow had overtaken his life. He became very rebellious and very negative. He was going out of control and I was still getting high. I wonder what it was ever going to take for me to see the damage I was causing to my family.
I was still in this deep dark hole; I cried Lord please help me. I cried from within me, no matter how much crack I did, God still had a hold on me. Deep down inside I still wanted to be free from this

substance controlling me. I didn't know that Jesus could Love someone like me.

As my son continue to rebel my education started to fail. I could see myself inside my son and this was not a good sight to see. It truly became unpleasing to me to see my son in such a way.
He was on the same road of destruction and we were going down together. This was now putting a strain on our relationship, and I was the blame. I could not be the mother he wanted me to be, I was ashamed of what and who I had become. It was now at a point I had to become accountable for our actions. Although it was the hardest thing one might have to do.

How long will we blame everyone but ourselves for our short comings in life? It's everybody else fault except our own. My son needed me and I was not able to help him because I needed help myself. I recall a time when a friend and I were walking; we were also with an older man who was willing to buy us some alcohol at the local store.  As we were walking the man told us he had not had a drink in 13 years; I replied I wish I could go 13 days without a drink.  It was at that point I realized that my desire to be free started to mean something to me.  It still wasn't my time yet, although I was not far from being free.   I still suffered a little while longer.  I didn't understand why; but I know why now.

God had a plan for me, I couldn't see it at the time but it was working out in my favor.  My brother and sister were saved and their lives where truly redeemed by the word of God.

 They would tell me to stop drinking and doing drugs.  I need to get my soul saved and redeemed by God's word.  Again I chose to abuse the drugs and drink my alcohol.  I didn't want to hear about being redeemed and God's salvation.

# Lifestyle of

## Destruction

This addiction had control of me and the
devils wanted to destroy my life.  He also
wanted to destroy my child.  If we think the
way we live doesn't affect our child, we are
definitely sick and truly wrong. We can
become a very negative force against our
children with very slim positive outcome.

Our children can constantly be affected in the
atmosphere of our dysfunctional life style
without our awareness until it's too late.  As
time went on I hear things about my son and
how he has started selling weed.   As I looked
at my son, I could see the problem in created

for his life. I cried, Jesus I need a change in my life. I need my life to be Redeem by the word God.

My son needed me so greatly and I wanted to be changed, but I still was under the control of this addiction. So we both continued down this path. Soon I got word my son had stolen someone's dope and they were looking for him, Oh my God! Please Lord, I hope they don't kill my son.

I went home to see if my son was there. I looked in his bedroom but he was not there. As I looked around in his room I noticed the window was open, I pulled back the curtains and there was a brick lying in the window. My heart immediately sank into my stomach. Where is my son, I feared what might of happen to him. I waited and wonder what was going on and where was my son until he finally came home. Thank God my son was okay. I looked at my son and I asked him about what happen and what he was doing?

I realized now I wanted to be free more now than ever. I was tired of the same old routine; day in and day out. I often wondered, is there a better life for a person such as me. I didn't know at the time that Jesus was listening to me. Then I found out how patience is Our God. He waited and he continues to wait on me. I begin to think about all the times I could have been dead and gone. I ask the Lord, Jesus please don't let me die in my blood and in my sins. Now I begin to worry about where I was going to spend eternity. Will I go to heaven or am I going to hell?

Still on the destructive path and still doing my addictive drugs but I didn't know Christ was drawing me nearer to him. I realized the thoughts of heaven and hell were weighing stronger on my mind and I needed to be saved NOW! You cannot come unto the Father except he draws you closer to him. Time still went on the same and I was pretty much in the same place of destruction, yet the door of hope was still open.

I recall on this particular day something different was happening, my son and I were at home. I told my son I going to prepare dinner he ask what time are we eating? I told him w will eat at 5:30 pm, he said he would be back at 5:30 pm and went out the door.

I begin to clean up and do my chores around the house. I then went to the store to pick up grocery for dinner. I returned home as I prepared our meal I begin to reflect on my life It was 1990; my son was 21 years old, all his youthful years where without me as his mother. Nevertheless it was a good day for me and I was doing something different other than getting high. As I got close to getting my meal completed, I wonder where my son was. He had not yet returned home. Late night had began to fall; where could he be? A mother knows when something is wrong when it comes to her child, I knew something wasn't right. I begin to worry but I continue to wait, I wanted him to come home and have his dinner. I was surprised of myself, I had not gone out. I didn't do my normal routine the things I would usually do. I realize worrying about my son overpowered the desire to get high.


It was nighttime and my son hadn't returned home. As I lay down for the night, there was a loud beating on the door. It was so loud it scared me, I jumped up and I knew immediately it was about my son.
I went to open the door there was a police officer and cruiser outside my house. The officer said," Mam, we are looking for Ricky Wilkerson", and I said, "he is not here, I have not seen him all day" then he said "May I come in and take a look around", as they approached inside my house, I begin to ask my questions, "What has he done? The officer

said, "He was involved in a robbery at the dairy mart and one police officer was shot, my next question, "Is the officer dead? He replied, "No, the officer was shot in the shoulder. I then asked, "Was my son the shooter he was with 3 other guys"

It was a great fear that had fell upon me, I allowed the officer to search my home for my son. He wasn't there as I had said to the officer earlier. All I could think is that my son didn't know what to do. If the police officer found him what would be the outcome? I was so fearful, I thought what if he run and they saw him, and this could force then to shoot him while in pursuit trying to catch him. As I lay back down to, I tried to sleep, but I couldn't sleep very well worrying about my son. Morning came; I called the police station to see if my son had been arrested. I was told that my son was in custody. I was relieved because he was not dead.

Later that day I went to the police station to visit my son, I was angry at him and at myself at the same time. I thought to myself what is going to take for me to be the mother that I should have been. I was not able to get my son out on bond. I don't think I would have,

because I know he was somewhere keeping out
of trouble and staying out of harm's way. I
also realize I knew where he was at. I found
out my son was with some guys from Chicago
and one of the guys from Chicago shot the
police officer in the shoulder. My son had the
gun that held up the robbery at dairy mart
and he was found guilty. He was in jail it was
time for sentencing. I visit my son regularly
but now I was on my way to court, I went to
the hearing for his sentencing; He was given 6
years. After serving two months in Prison I
was able to visit. I was so hard to see us
separate at the end of our visit. How could I
go on like this with my child in prison, what
could I do?

I went on using drugs and alcohol to cope with
my pain and the mess I had made of my life
and now I have to visit my son in prison.
Something change and I begin to pray from
within and I cried out unto the Lord. I cried
differently, Lord please change me. I prayed,
Lord Change me before my son come home
from prison; my change still had not yet come.
I recall asking Lord change me to be a mother
to my son and a person respectful in his life. I
wanted my son to see me in a better way. I
didn't want to be a person on drugs and

alcohol.  I wanted to be respected and
responsible and very productive.
As time went on I still continue to get high and
I still prayed, It seemed like the more I prayed
things still didn't get any better.  I didn't know
that I wasn't ready for this change that I had
been praying for in my life.  As time went on I
felt like it was at the end of my road.  I was so
miserable that I didn't know what to do.  I
wanted so much to be free of this life.

I wanted a different life when my son comes
home, if I could just have a better life.  But I
needed it for myself.  I continue to visit my son
and I struggled deeply with my addiction
because my son was serving 6 years now in
prison. I recall in 1991, I was out at the bar
and I had a few drinks which always lead to
another high in the form of drugs.
  I remember hearing a saying "One addiction
leads to another" and this is so true.  I went to
friend's house and we got together and bought
some crack cocaine and alcohol.  I was setting
things in place as normal to get high all day
and high all night.  It was close to Midnight
and I had gotten high as I could get.  I needed
to come down from my high only to go back up
to being high again.

I was so miserable at this point and I knew it; I only wanted to go home, I wanted to go to sleep and get away from myself. I had to babysit the next morning for my sister, so I began to walk home. I thank God it wasn't far to walk but it seem like forever. I was so high at this point I could hardly make it. My heart was beating so fast, it felt as though it was coming up out of my chest. I was tired and scared of how these drugs were destroying my life and killing my body. I needed a change in my life and I need now. I didn't want to stay this way, I can't make it this way, and something has to change.

# Chasing

# Jason

I began to call on the name of the Lord, I prayed to God a lot during my life of turmoil. But this time it was different, I found myself calling from my heart and not my lips. It was though I could see my heart come forth through my cry; it wasn't just words from my lips. When I prayed before I wasn't completely ready for such a change. At this point my whole life flashed before. I begin to think about all the things I could have done different. All the people I had hurt with my selfishness.

I couldn't go back and fix anything wrong I did it was too late for that. I was so ashamed of who I was, I didn't feel worthy of any help from any one. But I thank God for being merciful to those who call upon him. I begin to talk to the Lord on the inside and I prayed these words, "Lord I heard you could do anything, would you please take the taste of alcohol and drugs from me because I am so tired of me. I need you to change this life for me so that I can be a normal person. I want to live a life not controlled by alcohol and drugs" I continued to talk to the Jesus on my way home. I begin to desire a life of free from this addiction that was killing me. I could only hope that Jesus heard my plea. My life was like a movie of the worst kind, I had no way of escape; I couldn't even image to come out of this life. For me to fight this it was a nightmare, it was like "Friday the 13$^{th}$, and I was chasing Jason.

Jason was my every drug of addiction. A monster I created to live the life God gave to me. Everything that I could get high on from Heroin, crack cocaine, pills, alcohol and the people who carried these drugs of addictions, they became my way of life. It was me "Chasing Jason "a nightmare of the worst kind. Chasing the monster dragon, made up like a ghost, which became real in my mind. In my mind, it was in and out, up and down, my world swirled around; I was driven in circles of destruction and darkness of no end. I was paralyzed in this life; it was the way I thought to live.

I thought about my family and how this life had truly separated me from them. "Chasing Jason was a Life of destruction. Every morning I had to have a beer to start my day, then as the day progress checking in with my friend and the place where we always come to get high. After several hours of smoking weed, then getting high on crack cocaine, sometimes called "Girl", we would be on an ultimate high.

We had to find a way to come down; chasing Jason was every bit of a nightmare taking me stay to hell. I was bound to run this race going to hell "chasing Jason" I had to come down and I need my fix that came in that folded brown paper envelope, street name called "Boy' or "smack" known as heroin, a matted white powered, and when injected inside into the body, it converts into morphine . A world of delusion and a life of hell is what you pay. As I got close to home I realized that my life was in hell and my family and no one else could help me. At this point I had no thought of what to do nor did I have any idea how my life was about to change. As I finally reached home and got ready for bed. As I laid down with so many different emotions I was trying to find a grip on my life; I couldn't rest, it was something going on within me.

# Instamatic Change by the Grace of God

It was a strange feeling that came over me not knowing what the next day would bring. I set my alarm clock for my wake up time, so I could go and babysit for my sister who lived 20 minutes away. As I Laid down to rest; I was hoping and praying that God would change my life and I no longer use drugs and alcohol. The alarm went off; I woke up it was and it was morning. As I begin my day getting ready I knew something was different about today. After getting cleaned up and dress, I begin my walk to my sister's house. Normally as I walk I am thinking about drinking a six pack of beer waiting at my sister's house. But on this day the thoughts of beer was far from me. I didn't realize God was working on my behalf. God was getting ready to reveal things to me. As I got to my sister's house, I knocked on the door. My sister opens the door, she said, "Your beer is in the fridge" I said, "okay". I went to the fridge and open the door; I looked at the beer and I closed the door.

It was that day I never looked back, I never had another drink of alcohol; nor did I get high again on drugs. I was drug and alcohol free and it's been 22 years, I have never looked back. As that day continued, I begin to feel the change that had taken place in my life. My sister came home from work and saw the beer still in the fridge; I told her how I cried out and prayed to God to remove the taste of alcohol and drugs far from me.

It was next day and the desire for drugs and alcohol didn't come back. Now my family and I were so amazed at what God had done. We all knew how this drug and controlled my life. This addiction had destroyed me and the relationship with my family. But now the best thing that could have ever taken place in my life has happen to me, I am Drug Free.

This was the best thing ever to happen in my life, I had to tell everybody. I went to the places where I hung out drinking smoking and getting high; I wanted everyone to see what God had done for me.


As I went to these places where I had been drinking and getting high Go had now delivered me and I didn't get high again. God had truly answered my prayer. As time went passed I still babysit for my sister and I begin to embrace the change in my life. God had given me a new life and I was ready to life like a new born baby. There were so many wonderful new things in my life because I was free from drugs. I was no longer control by the negative influence of any drugs.

Waking up every morning was a new thing in my life, I was drug-free. My morning was not open with a bottle or can of beer. At noon time I didn't have to smoke a marijuana cigarette; nor shoot up my arms with anything I could get my hands on. All this new living without drugs had completely changed my life. It was like a makeover and the mask had been removed. At last I could breathe each moment without drugs and live a fresh new life. I took a deep deep breathe and exhaled. It felt like freedom. The chains had came off that had me in bondage it was so much good happening in my life, yet something was still missing I had not been saved and I felt as though I needed to commit my life to the Lord. There was another change about to take place inside of me. I recall my feelings; it was like a thirst and a hunger going on inside of me. I needed to get close to Jesus in such a way I was one in him. I wanted to spend eternity with Jesus in my life. I didn't want to go to hell; I was getting this strong hunger and desire for the Lord. I couldn't think about nothing else, it was a burning desire deep inside of me. I didn't know this was God drawing me. As I continued on daily in my new life, I prayed to God for my soul to be saved.

It was in the summer of 1992, I was at a revival where my sister attended church. It was a Revival that the Church had every year in the month of July. Every year my sister would always invite me to come to this revival It was though I was waiting on this time to come but the devil never allowed me to get here. I was still in a battle with the devil in my Mind. I heard a voice say wait until next week, so I waited. After a few days of waiting, it was Sunday night and I tried to lie down to sleep, but I heard the Lord, you may not make till next week.
So then I called my sister, I asked her would she take me down to the church to with the pastor. She said no one was at the church, it was too late. Then my heart dropped, it was broken; I was so angry. I felt as though my sister had let me down, but I didn't know my life was in God's hands. I begin to pray askin God to let me make it to revival on Monday. I was willing to give up all my ways to find Jesus. My heart wanted Jesus inside no matter what it took, even if it took my life. Jesus said you can't come to the father unless he draws you.

I was so glad God had drawn me unto him. So as the night went on I prepared for bed. I didn't sleep very well that night, longing for the break of dawn. I got up early that morning, because I had to babysit for my sister; I was so glad to see this day. I still had a chance to pray to God to have my soul saved. I didn't want to go to hell. I had to get close unto the Lord.

As I prepared to get ready to go my sister, which was not a far where I lived; I would always walk. I begin walking to my sister; it was as though no one else was in the world but me and Jesus. I wanted so much at that time to be born again and to free my life complete from sin.

As I reached my sister I started my day, asking my sister to please take me to revival tonight. She said, "Yes" and my sister went to work. I continued in prayer about my soul being saved. I recall my days being different as I attended the laundry and others duties as I cared for my niece and nephew while them playing. I felt as though my life was about to change.

The day went on and my sister returned home from work and we begin to get ready for revival. All day long it seems as though the weight of the world was on my shoulder. The

69

heaviness of sin and shame from the things I had done somehow had weighed me down. When I got to church I sat on the front row seat with the other sinners.

As I thought to myself I finally made it, as I sa there people who were saved where giving their testimony about how Jesus saved their soul. Then the pastor begins to explain the plan of salvation unto God. As we seat on the front row bench, which is the mourning bench for sinners who want their souls to be saved during the time of revival.

I continue to seat on the seat and listen to the pastor and I am calling on Jesus to have merc on me, I could feel him at the door of my hear and I needed to let him in. The service had come to an end for that night and I hadn't got saved. I felt as though I wasn't worthy enoug and my life was not worth living. But I still prayed to Jesus to have mercy on me.

I went home that night; all I could think abou is where I was going to spend eternity. You see I knew there was a hell and didn't want to go there. So I begin to pray and ask the Lord if he was going to save my soul. I wanted to know so I asked him to wake me up at midnight because I wanted my soul to be saved.

As I prepared for bed, I fell asleep for a short time; I remembered what I had asked the Lord to do for me. Well as I woke up the first thing I did was look at the clock, guess what time it was, it was Twelve O'clock midnight. The reason I ask God for this because the pastors said, you can ask the Lord, show you a sign if you are on the right road to salvation. I know the Lord had showed me a sign but that old devil tried to tell me you were going to wake up at midnight anyways. I didn't believe that devil because I knew what I had asked the Lord. I choose to believe in the word of God not the words of the devil. I had a different way of thinking and I choose to follow what I desired in my heart. It takes a little faith in God in order to receive salvation. The next morning, I'll never forget it was August 4th, 1992, that day I received salvation unto the Lord. It was the day the Lord had made and prepared just for me. I remember this day like it was just yesterday and my New life was about to begin.

It was a Tuesday morning and I'm walking to my sister it was though my life was on a one way path and I had to make to my destination it was truly a different atmosphere that day. I was babysitting for my sister and I continued to call on the Lord, I didn't know anything else to do but to keep praying unto the Lord. All day long I prayed and prayed, as time drew closer for my sister to come home from work; I was ready for tonight's revival at church.

When we got to church that night I sat on the same seat as the night before. I was crying inside, Lord please have mercy on me. As the pastor was preaching the word of God, it was though he was only speaking to other sinners and I was getting angry. I felt angry rising up because he wasn't paying me any attention; I know the devil had put those thoughts in my head. I still had a fight going on in my mind with satan; he didn't want to let me go.

As I remember all of this, it was at the end of service on that Tuesday night, the pastor said, "Faye, I dare you to call on the name of the Lord until you die" In my heart, I said finally he said something to me. I responded in my heart to the Lord, this is the time to tell you I will call on your name until I die. I begin to say what the pastor told me to say, "I going to call on your name Lord until I die" immediately it was though I was connected directly to God.

I remember telling the Lord I wasn't going anywhere until he changed my life. I told the

Lord to get it over with because I was ready to die to live for him. You have to lay your life down for the Lord and lose yourself in order to live for God. The Lord said unto me, if I try to save my life I would lose it, but if I give my life unto him I would have life eternally.
It was right then when this transformation in my life was about to take place. I recall the feeling of heaviness leaving my life, I felt so light at this point I could fly away. It was that heavy load of sin being lifted and my life being transformed. This was the power of God stirring up the Holy Spirit inside of me. It was 10:30pm and suddenly I saw a light from heaven shining through the window of the church. In this light I could see the saints from the church and I saw myself in this light. I was no longer in darkness; I was in the marvelous light of God.
I was in the presence of God and I knew I was in his Powerful light. The power of God had filled me with Joy unexplainable. I was full of God's Glory, all I could do was say "thank you Jesus", I praised the Lord and continued to thank him. I praise him over and over and over again I knew I had been born again. At that point I had no more doubt about what had happen, I knew I had been born again and the devil couldn't do anything about it.

God is so real and Salvation is freely given.  H
is a kind and merciful God to those who call
upon his name.  I am so glad I called Jesus.
There is power in the name of Jesus because
now I am free from bondage. My life that was
bound in sin is no longer bound anymore.  I
have been completely transformed and I have
a new life to live.

# A REDEEMED LIFE

I was on a new path and I realize I had new ideas coming into my mind. I started thinking I needed a job because my sister's boys were reading for pre-school and I was not needed to babysit anymore. I realize it was time to be more productive in my life

I decide to apply for my driver's license; I was 39 and I didn't have a license to drive. I had saved enough money from babysitting to buy me a car and seek employment. I remember hearing about a job position at a nursing home; I went to apply for this job.

As I put in my application for the job; I was praying deep inside my soul; Lord please let me have this job. I filled in the application and returned it to the lady in personnel. She begin to ask me questions and one of the questions was can you start next week? My answer was yes!

I left the place praising God from my mouth all the way home. This was the beginning of many doors opening over my life. While on my new J job I remembered seeing the face of someone working there who knew me when I was caught up in addiction. I remember hearing them tell someone about my drug addiction, I could hear every word that was said. I then decide to tell them my testimony, how God delivered me from alcohol and drugs addiction.  God has saved my soul and I'll never be the same.  He transformed my life and redeemed from the pit of hell, I am not the same person anymore; I have a new life in Jesus.

I worked at my Job in the nursing home for 4 years.  Then I began a new job at the radio station.   A friend mentions my name to the owner at the radio station.  I was called in by the owner for an interview and things went well for me.  I was hired at the radio station making much more money.   My Job detail was cleaning certain area of the station and I enjoyed my work and did a very good job.

I began to meet lots of great people; I worked there for over 6 years but I didn't health benefits. Therefore I began to look elsewhere for employment.  I needed a job that would offer me health benefits.   I got a job at Procto and Gamble through a temp service. I worked more hours and I had health benefits.  I worked as a line worker putting detergent bottles in boxes.

I caught on pretty fast, but the work was different with longer hours and a dress code. had worn steel toed boots that were very uncomfortable.   I been promoted on my job and I continue to do well.  I thought about my sister concerning a job, she had been working at the hospital for many years. I asked my sister if they were hiring and she said she would let me know. My sister work in Dietary and I also knew a friend who worked in housekeeping.

Again I began to pray and ask God to open a door for at the hospital. God heard my pray and provided for me. He provided for me in every way he did not let me want for nothing. This was all new for me and it seemed so unreal.

So many good and wonderful things happening in my life; I was overwhelmed with what God was doing in my life. It was better that I could ever imagine. I never was as sure of anything as I am of serving such a loving God.

I now wanted to get my G.E.D and I knew God would direct my path. I realized now I had to study in order to past my G.E.D test. After studying and preparing over a year I was ready to take my test. I prayed to God in confidence and yes I passed; now I had my G.E.D.

for chemical high.  I tried everything from marijuana to heroin stealing from friends and family blind in the process.  I made several attempts to get myself out of the hole I was in, but I failed every time.

Then one night, I cried out to Jesus to help me out of my madness. When I got up the next morning, it was a different day for me.  I was able to think clearly, I realized I alone was responsible for the choices I had made.  No one else decided for me.  And it saddened me that have mistreated myself and others so badly.

I realized I had deprived myself of a normal life as a young adult.  I got a late start on everything.  Now I have my driver's license, my G.E.D and have been working productively for the past 17 years.  I thank God for the opportunity he has given me.  I never imagined I would be where I am today.  Through it all, my family stood by me.  My church supported me.  My new friends encouraged me.  My message is that there is hope regardless of who we are.  God delivered me and he is still able to deliver.  Remember, good choices bring life."  Those were my words that were written in the Newspaper. I also remember someone else in the community who was making a difference his statement was also printed in the paper. It was a strong titled to the statement of what this brother had to say, "Drugs bring Death bringing a change" written by Jesse Lowe a brother in the community. His statement reads as, "I am just a vessel bringing awareness of the drug problem surrounding our city since March 31; Drug Bring death has been able to help many people. Seven people have been placed in rehab; six people who did not have a job are working. One has accepted Christ as his savior.

Businesses in Lima have joined us in properly training addicts to deal with recovery. Unity Elementary School has a new pilot program. This program will train and educated children to make wiser choices in life, build bonds between the child and the parent, and develop a friendship among the teachers and neighbors.

Eleven public stands, one public march, two citywide meetings and 18 speaking appearance later, we're still going strong.

We are now a 501(c)3 status. We are trying to make a difference in this great city. Two chapters have started in Alabama.

"Drugs Bring Death", believes death comes from the use and abuse of drugs: spiritually, mentally and physically.  We believe people who stand together stay together, because there is power in numbers.
It also allows the neighbors of the city to learn to speak to each other and fellowship among one another, once we can learn to talk to one another, and then we can learn work together

Look at God work in my life; I give God all the credit.  I know I couldn't have done any of this without God; there was no way these things would happen unless God was in my life.   I am so amazed how God took nobody like me, who was on the road of destruction and he turned my whole life around.  I have been given a new life; the bible say to be in Christ you become a new creature and behold all things are new.  I know this to be true, because this happened to me.
I have had some hearts and pains while on this Christian Journey.  As I look back on the memories I endure.   I recall losing two brothers and sister, it broke my heart knowing they have passed on but God has kept me through it all.  There is true conform knowing they were saved.  I can see them in heaven.

Truly my live didn't start until Jesus saved my soul. I removed the mask from my face and now I can breathe. The breath of God has given me new life and I'll never be the same. I didn't become the woman that I am until I met Jesus in my life. My life is not on any shaky ground today; Jesus is a solid foundation, in him my life is Redeem. I'm standing on that solid rock called Jesus. I can see my life has been set free. Whom the son set free is free indeed. My life is so full of benefits and rewards. I can't keep it to myself, what God has done for my life I have to tell somebody. I want others to know God has power to change your life if you only believe.

When you become a believer and life is redeemed you won't be the same. I asked God to redeem my life and I asked in the Name of Jesus. Then as I begin to ask I learn to believe. Though I may not always get my answers right away I still believe. God is always answering my prayers.
It's not the end but a new beginning God has allowed me to achieve. Some things that I have dreamed about in my adduction he has open doors for me to accomplish, it was a dream that has now become an opportunity happening in my life. I have this opportunity

to share how I have overcome the struggle of addiction and become the person I only once dreamed I would ever become. My life is very rewarding and I give Glory and honor to God Today In this year I will be turning 62 year old. I so please to have made it thus far in my Life.

I thought my life would have ended so much sooner, but God has kept my life this far So many simple things in life we take for granted never thought I would apply for neither pension nor social security from working a job. What God gave me was a productive prosperous Life drug free. I came what day a a time, but it came. As I now set my life in position to retire from a Job, never did I dream to live my life this far. Shame on me, I had choose to stay in the grips of addictions for so long, I was so far out of touch with the responsibility of life. Yet now my life has been redeemed and I can see differently.
Not being afraid of hard work and getting an education that can build a productive life. I am steady striving to give my best to God that I may be my best. I am so satisfied with this new redeemed Life that God has given unto me; I can hardly remember that old person whom I used to be. I so Bless I must tell other

of this New redeem Life I live.  Because of the different health issue of my family member I have suffered much loss.  I have lost loved ones such as my two brothers, and my sister; I never looked back to use the drugs that once destroyed my life but for the Grace of God who kept me through it all I am still Redeemed.

*William Wilkerson (Pig)*

**Remembering my two Brothers and sister, they were well known in the community. They were full of life with big hearts full of love and laughter. They will never be forgotten.**

**James Otis Wilkerson (Bubble)**

*Sharon Boult*

I had to share my testimony and tell of my life experiences; I have to let others know about this grip of addiction and the redemption of Jesus Christ our Lord and savior.

I recall a time when I *was able to share my testimony:*

### My testimony was about
### Wanting Jesus More Than Anything"

It was the year 2006, it was at the Elm Street of the Brethren is gav my testimony to in the fellowship of this church congregation "I thought I would be a junky all my life" But then I met Jesus and everything changed.

I was on a road of destruction through most of my life" From about to 38 years of age I lived a life of heroin, cocaine, and meth. I put i in my body any way I could get it in there. Then I got tired."

I used to live a block from the church in my neighborhood that wou place a vinyl bag of information hanging on my doorknob, yet I nev pay any attention.

Then one day an older man I knew told me he had not drink in thirteen years, I could only think to myself I wish I could not drink for thirteen days.

Soon after, I was high, walking home to lie down,"

Every day I babysit for my sister, "she always had to have six-pack i the fridge or I wouldn't do it", but the next morning was different The first I did was go to the refrigerator and the beer was there, bu couldn't even touch it. "Since that day I have had none". "I've ha no drugs or alcohol, I didn't have withdrawals and I don't have a desire. I asked the Lord to take this taste from my mouth and he did

92

"My friends couldn't understand." "What are you going to do now?" They asked me, "I'm going to get in church, that what I told them, I wanted Jesus more than anything.

Nine months later, my sister told me about revival meetings at her church. 'I decide to go, there was a guy there who got saved and he had been on drug just like me."

"This guy was praising Jesus and I was getting upset'. I told the Lord you got to save me."

"I went home, but I couldn't rest. I kept begging the Lord to save my soul". "It was Sunday night, and I called my sister to take me down to the church and she said there is no one theirs, it's too late, she said ". I was restless all night, "I babysat the next day and went to revival that night. My Friend was praising the Lord and I was sitting on the front mourner's bench. I went home again that night and went again Tuesday night. It was at the end of the service the pastor invited anyone who wanted to prayer all night to come up to the front." "I remember the pastor saying, Faye, I dare you tell the Lord I'm going to call you till I die, and I started saying that". I felt like I weighed a ton that night.

"I felt like want to live anymore." I remember, "I wanted to change, I wanted to get it over with". Then I heard a voice, say "Tell God to kill you, but I couldn't get it out". The next thing I knew I was on the floor." "I couldn't get up". I stretched out my hand and I felt the Lord pulling me up". "I thanked the Lord"

"The Lord God is real, there is no trickery about this" God put his hands on me. I'm here to tell you that God is real as sure as I am standing here. All of us have things we can't handle. "We just need to give them to him, I didn't want to live the way I was, but I didn't know what else to do. I'm just thankful he didn't' turn his back on me."

I asked the Lord, Am I ever going to be a responsible human being? "Now I thank God that he has allowed me to have a job". I was 40 years old when I got my driver's License." I realize later how much darkness I was really in. "He put his love in me and I fell in love with People I didn't even know." Now I want to be more like Christ.

I have learned to wait on the Lord, because he knows what I need and when I need it. There is nothing to hard for God, he can do anything but fail. I was able it give my testimony because God allowed it. I was at the "Elm Street Church' in my city. I told my testimony and some of the people came up to me and asked more questions about my life and how Jesus changed me.

Everyone needs to know God is willing and able to give new life. A life free from drug addiction, alcohol and anything that keeps you bound in sin. God loves us so much he gave his only begotten son so you can be free. I am here now 23 years clean and sober. God kept me all those years; I am now confident I will continue to walk in spirit of Christ Jesus. I shall walk in a life redeemed by the word. He paid a price for my salvation that I may have life eternally.

I will never be able to live my life without the power of the Holy Spirit living within me. I am honored to be kept by God and redeem by his wonder working power.

My Life did not end but God forgave me and now my life begins. The blood that Jesus shed for me was the price he paid for my life. Jesus Christ who went to Calvary for the sins of this old world. He knew no sin but yet he died for this whole world to be sin free. Let Jesus redeem your life and you live your life sin free In Jesus Name. I have a beautiful family whom I cherish and I'll praise God for what he has done in my life.

*My younger sister, Patricia spoke about my life being changed and how it has made a difference, she said, "Sometimes it was a real struggle looking after my nephew. But we did WHAT we had to do. My sister Diane and I made sure he had clothes ON HIS back, Food to eat and a roof over HIS head. He was our priority especially around the holidays. Even though he loved HIS Mother so much it was hard to MAKE him understand WHY we couldn't let go WITH her sometimes. I was ALWAYS in denial About the Things my sister Faye was doing i just didn't*

96

*want to BELIEVE none of it. Seeing her ON drugs is WHAT kept me away from them.*

 *"When my sister got saved in 1992, I saw an awesome change in her. Especially when she didn't want to do any of the old things she used to do. She has an amazing love for the LORD After Seeing all that she went through before she got saved"*

My sister Dee Dee wrote a very special letter to me on my birthday, I realize she would never speak these words directly to me but she wrote them on paper and I'll never forget what she wrote.

# The Letter'

I remember a letter I received from my sister
Dee Dee, she said in the letter "Well Carolyn
you made the big sixty, "thank God for you.
You been here for me a long time trying to be
my mother and that's fine but you know Caro
what was what , but Carol I just wanted to say
just looking back over the years where you
been and where you are going, I been there for
it all.  I just want you to know you had a
struggle. But you made it.  Because I thought
you wouldn't make it, but God knew best.  He
saw your ups and downs.  Faye through it all
you made it we had hard times we had bad
times but we made it.  As Pig would say
"Golden girls" Bubbles say, "Crip", Pat would
say "Now", and Sharon would say "Carol" an
you know what I would say.
I just wanted to take this time out to say
"Thank You'. for being here for me when I
needed you.  It wasn't always peaches and
cream, but I expect. That because we were
always able to talk to one another even when
we were mad at each other.   We didn't stay
mad at each for days or weeks at a time life to
short for that, I just want to say Carol I LOV
YOU no matter what.  Wish I could be the so
"LADY TAKE A BOW YOU DESERVE IT"

# "Redeemed "

God you saw in me something that was
worth redeeming, you saw something
that I could not see, that goes to show
you know who far I could not see.
For I did not know that there was
redemption for me, through thee.
My God how could you see any worth in
me.
For all I see is this destruction that has
taken over me.
So tell me how you could see any worth
in me, for I went against all that you said
I should be.
I heard that you love me, so much that
you gave your son for me, a ransom for
my life.

Now as I attempt to call on thee, just to see if you will come and redeem me.
Lord please come and redeem me from this destruction that has control of me, because you my child have asked, because of the love that I and my son have for you.
I made you in my image therefore I saw me in you.
I had to redeem that which belongs to me.
So I paid the price with the life, of my son Jesus Christ

I am Woman of God and a Friend to my sister
Carolyn Faye Wilkerson. We have shared
many similar stories and travel many of the
same paths here in the city of Lima Ohio. I
have volunteered and served with her and I
know she has a story to tell and I she has much
knowledge to offer to others who struggle with
drug addiction and a loss of loved ones.
She has a powerful anointing on her life and a
love for Jesus that is transforming. I also

have learned from her humble ways and sincere spirit.

God is with my sister, Carolyn and she is called to serve and help other to overcome their struggle of drugs and alcohol wherever she travels. Her desire to open homes and community centers to service women who are fighting the struggle of drugs and life depressions for loss and setbacks in their lives I am honor to serve and learn from my sister such wisdom and humility that I have witnessed on her journey.

I encourage all to take time and read her stor and gain hope for a redeemed live in Jesus name.

Prophetess Evangelist Felecia Spaulding
Publish Author, Actress, Psalmist

# Obituary

Mable Lee Boult, my mother would be welled-please with the outcome of her children's lives today. My mother obituary reads as follow:

Maple Lee Boult, daughter of Milton Butler and the late Mrs. Julie Bulls Bulter, was born in Center Star, Alabama, November 26,1927 and departed and departed from this life on February 14th, 1970 at the age of 42years 7 months and 2 days.

Her younger life spent in Florence Alabama where she attended the public schools and

churches, about the age of13 she professed her
belief in God and joined the Cumberland
Presbyterian church.  In 1948 she was united i
holy matrimony to Mr. Lloyd Wilkerson in
Louisville, Kentucky and to this union 5
children was born.  In 1958she moved her fam
to Lima, Ohio where she was later married to
Mr. Clyde E. Boult about 1962 and gave to thi
union one child was born.


She leaves to mourn their loss 4 daughters:
Carolyn Faye, Patricia, Diana Wilkerson and
Sharon Boult all at home.  2sons: William
Thomas Wilkerson, now station with US army
and James Otis Wilkerson at home. Her father
Milton Butler, also of Lima.  One sister, Mrs.
Bessie Turner of Buffalo, New York. And One
brother: Arthur Butler of Lima and one
grandchild; Ricky Wilkerson.  Numerous othe
relatives and a host of friends and
acquaintances

Made in the USA
San Bernardino, CA
11 November 2015